inking bitterns

poems and pictures for wild places

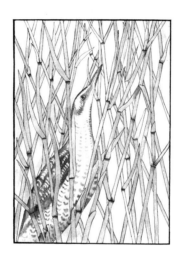

inking bitterns

poems and pictures for wild places

illustrated by Dru Marland

Bristol

Gert Macky Books
mmxiii

first published in 2013 by
Gert Macky Books
6 Belvedere Rd, Bristol, BS6 7JG
drusilla.marland@btopenworld.com
gertmacky.co.uk

printed by minutemanbristol.com

ISBN 978-0-9926783-1-9

to Katie, who is pretty wild

inking bitterns

song

my
spill
and
sky
the
touch
I
until
ascent
vertical
a
on
joy
my
take
I

Skylark
Alauda arvensis

Liz Brownlee

Kin

Every November they gather together,
raggedy black with petroleum sheen
and sparks in their feathers.

Most live local,
drifting from suburbs like bonfire smoke,
although others hurl in from further afield,
storming up songlines,
until, like a genie freed from a lamp,
they swirl and set the sky alight
with their crackling dance.

A parliament of starlings,
cacophonous cousins,
an argumentation of uncles and aunts!

Then one venerable elder
hunches his shoulders, opens his throat
and lets fly a hymn in notes
grown richer over years,
swelled by a hundred kindred voices,
all singing in different keys
their shared story.

Deborah Harvey

Bedtime Story

little piggy
little piggy
let me come in

wolf at the door/wolf at the window/wolf on the
roof/wolf down the chimney

the sky is falling, the sky is falling

but it was only the rain falling through the roof
again.

My little boy and I blew up his paddling pool and
we caught the wolf OK.
This was 10.30 p.m. on a Thursday.
With the help of buckets and bowls and plastic
sheeting we captured most of his noisy children
too.

(It would have been nice to light a fire
to change the wolves into steam
but we had no coal for the same reason we
had no shelter from the rain that is the
wolves at the door and all around us)

My little boy couldn't sleep because of the noise
the wolves made falling into the buckets so he went
to sleep at my friend's. (The wolf hasn't found her
yet)

Alana Farrell

Botaurus stellaris

The morning rose in hope
and watched patiently from the field edge
over the mist-stilled lake
for a glance, but no:
too veiled in camouflage
to be found by chance.

Then silence collapses:
the eeriest of calls,
the echo is love.

Stewart Carswell

Calling The Collie

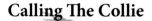

after Seamus Heaney

To choose a collie for a pet
is a decision you'll regret
unless you throw his manky ball
way beyond the lark's high call
and 'fore he grabs it in his jaws
(this is one of those iron laws)
these collie callings you must say,
then your word he will obey.

'The collie, call him braveheart,
teddyboy, brazen-tart,
the collieshangie, the please-don't,
the foot-pad, the raggle taggle – Oh!

Drawn by Dru, bandit-masked,
start-a-riot, stinky-poo.

The waltzer, the reeler,
the jigger, the moonlight-flitter,
the laldy-lad, the nimblewit.

The muck-tub, the bark-at-owt,
the out-like-a-rat-thru-the-crack-in-the-door,
the gad-about, the poky-snout.

The on-guard, the harum-scarum,
the sudden snap, the hurly-burly,
the sniffer, the busy-nose,
the ouija-nose, the blackguard,
and don't forget the pond-plunger.

The pink-panter, the lolling tongue,
the fizzog-licker, the twitchy-tail,
the country-dog, the beggar-boy,
the wear-you-down, the blagger,
the lightning-fork, the zigzagger,
the rebel with four paws, the tussock-nuzzler,
the dark-straggler, the light-smuggler,
the come-on, the hustler,
the toothy-smile, the come-and-go,
the glory-smile, the come-hither,
the bonny-beck, the watter-guzzler.

The pie with four legs, the bonny-so-braw,
the midnight-tune, the poem-on-the-moor,
the sweet disarmer,
the lovely darling,
the good-boy,
the beautiful boy.

The little-bastard! the spin-around,
the have-a-row, the go-to-ground
the doesn't-he-look-like-he's-laughing-at-you?

The belter between the bog and the bull,
the mirthfulling into the wonderful,
the joyfulling under the sun,
the blissfulling into his calling.'

If you can get all this said in time
the collie and you will be in rhyme.
And from this collielicious day
yourself he'll never disobey.
And if you really believe that's true
then all I can say is dog bless you.

Colin Brown

Redwings

Outside my window
a flock of angels
feasting on the pyracantha's
red berries.

Old devil blackbird,
whose territory this is,
frozen
on the garage roof,
in shock
or helpless rage –
longing for a shotgun
(who can tell?)

A warmth of feathers
colouring icy air:
Brown shading into brown –
brown set against cream;
sudden blush of red ochre.
And throat to tail
brush-speckled
water colour
on hand-made paper.

Angels,
dining on the pyracantha.

Only the blackbird
rejoiced
when they left –
sharp accountant's eye
on the remaining berries.

His evening song
longer
than usual.

John Terry

New Passage

So white a bird, the egret sails
Serene above the Severn mud
That smirches us, but can't assail
So white a bird; the egret sails.
Our boots sink in; we flounder, flail.
We'd rise and follow, if we could,
So white a bird. The egret sails
Serene above the Severn mud.

Dru Marland

14

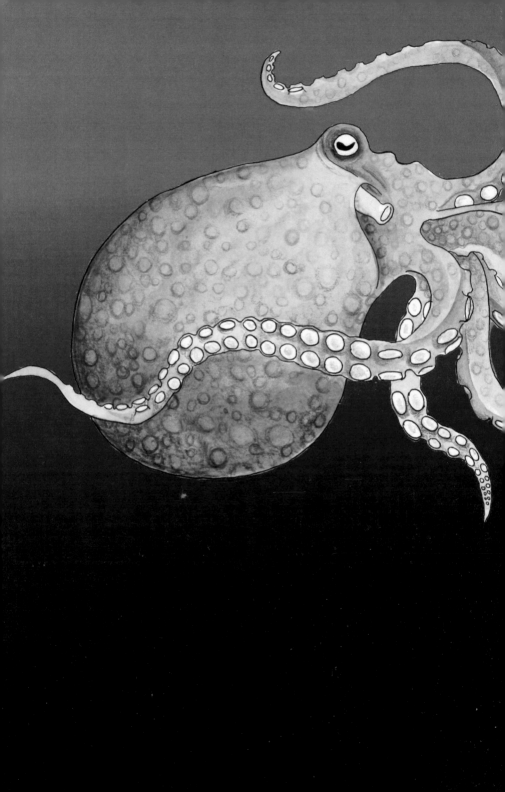

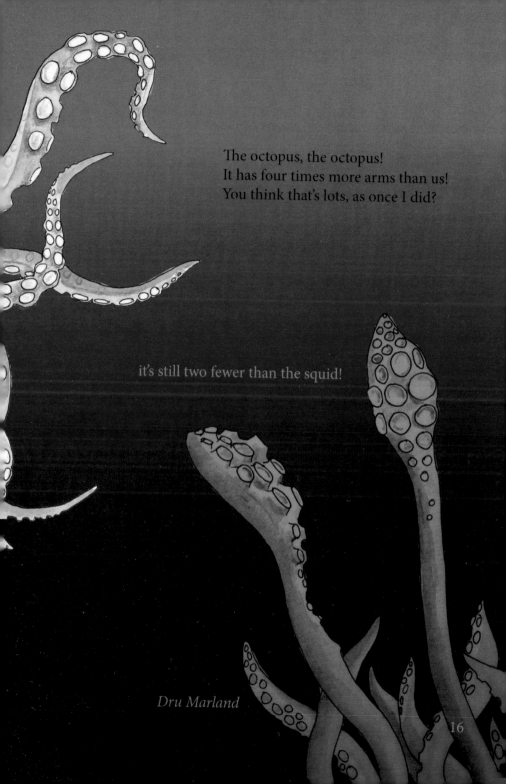

The octopus, the octopus!
It has four times more arms than us!
You think that's lots, as once I did?

it's still two fewer than the squid!

Dru Marland

16

virgin snow
a fox makes prints
for the morning

Alan Summers

I See You

I see you, says the shivering cat
to the wind that ruffles her fur.
Your fingers are blue, your face is fat
and you rush around without a hat.
I see you, says the shivering cat,
and turns her back and will not purr.
I see you, says the shivering cat,
to the wind that ruffles her fur.

John Terry

Outlaws

Hard to ignore the crows –
if only they would let me in

to the secrets of outlaw existence
the art of ragged wings.

I wish I could strut like a magpie
and switch my tail at the world

be the neighbourhood meddler
a confident heckler

and to hell with bad omens
and good reputations.

Cathy Wilson

Driving John Home

for JT

If we'd set out with intent, licked a finger, held it up
to tell which way the equinoctal wind was blowing,
hunkered under midnight's coats,
out of range of those long, preternaturally
sensitive snouts

If we'd adopted some disguise,
engaged the complicity of trees,
my hair dishevelled, snagged on twigs,
the cap you'd have donned to stymie moonshine
wreathed with ghosts of broken leaves

If we'd watched a warrior tribe creep
circumspectly from its sett, rootling for worms in fern
and raking grubs from bark with iron claws,
such an encounter couldn't have been
any more extraordinary

than our glimpse of badgers momentarily
frozen to the tarmac of Parry's Lane,
who trot into view when I close my eyes,
fossick through my dreams.
I should not be astounded.

Brocks are native to these parts,
their pads remember lost, obliterated tracks.
Yet in that instant, with hairy serendipity,
they were moon-snared Muses
excavating poetry.

Deborah Harvey   24

summer wind
a sparrow re-rights itself
at the peanut cage

Alan Summers

Grwyne Fawr

Sheep have spread their shrunken
woollens on barbed wire fences,
wisps bleached white by winter sun
imitating lichen hung on blackthorn
twigs to dry.

Delighted by pattern
the wind sends a pair of ravens overhead.
It thinks they sound like frogs
but to me it's clear that they are
deep in conversation

their topic a worsening in the weather,
the move of the livestock market
from Abergavenny to Raglan.
Or so I imagine,
not speaking raven.

Deborah Harvey

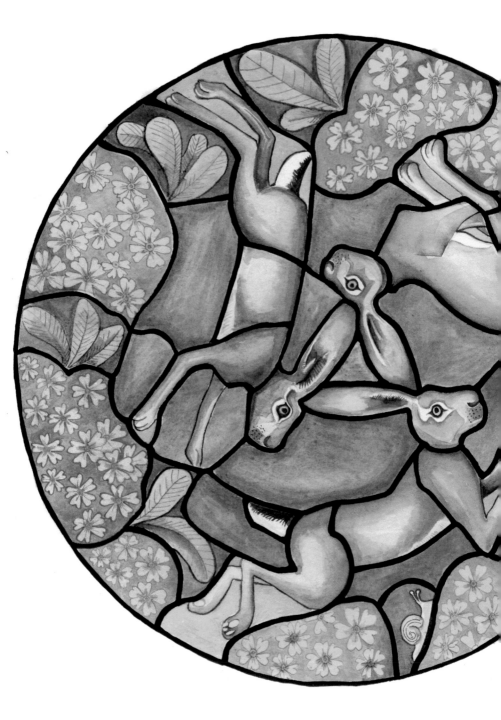

Full Circle

In ancient China
the moon is made of figured silk,
woven with the pattern of galloping hares,
three conjoined by a single ear,
together whole.

An eternal circle
embroidered on bolts of cloth,
carried by camel through singing sands,
the booming dunes of wind-whipped
Xhiang Sha Wan,

where Silk Road
frays to quick oasis, and
wondering artists paint three hares
on sacred temple cavern walls.
The Buddha's wheel

of life and death
rolls through Persia's burning plains,
eclipses sere, salt-desert suns: a brazen tray
engraved with hares, a stamped,
Islamic copper coin.

Crossing rivers, bridging rifts
in hidden groves of moss and stone,
these three hares chased on Jewish tombs
and makeshift tabernacle roofs,
the blackened beams

of Dartmoor churches
at the edges of the earth, bear
a trinity of hares, three in one, the risen son,
beneath a moon that pins
the universal oceans.

Deborah Harvey

Landfall

As splash is bracing, so's the daffodil's yellow;
Salt-sharp, and waxy to the touch;
First lighthouse loom, that longed-for landfall
after much wandering winter oceans.

Later, mellow on the Bristol train, my holdall stuffed
With Coptic crosses from Djibouti, buddhas from Colombo,
I watch the Wylye valley's willows roll
Slowly to the breeze's brush;
The roebuck, stilled mid-field to watch our passing;

And, on that bare bank, at last is such
A spray of primrose, petal pool of cream,
As glows against the stormcloud massing
Over the Plain; moment of grace

Warm as this sun now on my face,
Through the open window where I lean
To hear the evening-drowsy blackbird's song;
"Made it, though. Made it through another one."

Dru Marland

acknowledgements

Liz Brownlee's *Skylark* was first published in *Animal Magic*, IRON Press, 2011

Deborah Harvey's poems *Full Circle* and *Kin* were first published in her collection *Communion* (Indigo Dreams, 2011). *Kin* won the Dor Kemmyn Poetry Prize, 2011. *Driving John Home* was first published in *The Listening Walk* (Bath Poetry Café, 2013). *Grwyne Fawr* is part of the sequence *Speaking Raven* which won the 2013 Gloucestershire Prize (Buzzwords).

Alana Farrell's *Bedtime Story* first appeared in the magazine *Doors* (published by Words and Action, Dorset, 1989)

John Terry's *Redwings* was first published in *City* (Paralalia) and in *Wildlife* magazine

Alan Summer's *fox haiku* Publications credits: Hailstone Haiku Circle Japan (Japan 2010); *a little help from my friends* (Red Dragonfly ePamphlet 2011); *The Haiku Calendar 2012* (Snapshot Press); *fox dreams* ed. Aubrie Cox (April 2012): Award credits; Runner Up, The Haiku Calendar Competition 2011 (Snapshot Press): *sparrow haiku* Publications credits: *Snapshots 10* (2004); *tinywords* (2007); *Wing Beats: British Birds in Haiku* (Snapshot Press 2008); *Haiku Friends Vol. 3*, ed. Masaharu Hirata (Japan 2009)

the contributors

Colin Brown lives in Bristol. He is director of Poetry Can. His poem *Calling The Collie* was inspired by a border collie called Ted who belongs to the poet and novelist Deborah Harvey. It is written after Seamus Heaney's poem: *The Names of the Hare.*

Liz Brownlee lives near Bristol, writes for adults and children, and visits schools to talk and read poetry about endangered animals, the subject of her book, *Animal Magic.*
poetliz@mac.com, http://www.poetlizbrownlee.co.uk or http://www. animalmagicpoems.com

Stewart Carswell lives in Bristol where he is currently studying for a PhD in Physics. His poems are influenced by music, landscapes, and the manner of scientific exploration, and have been published in *Obsessed with Pipework* and *The Delinquent.*

Alana Farrell was born in Manchester to Polish and Ukrainian parents, and lives in Bristol, where her son was born, telling stories and writing. She is influenced by the wild, including fairytales and science fiction. Publications include *Other Poetry* and *The SHOp.*

Deborah Harvey lives in Bristol. Her first poetry collection, *Communion*, was published by Indigo Dreams in 2011 and her novel, *Dart*, in 2013. Her second collection, *Map Reading for Beginners*, will be published in 2014. Deborah enjoys hill-walking and making things out of glass.

Dru Marland is a sometime mariner, illustrator and aspiring poet, when she is not fixing bicycles and her Morris Traveller.

Alan Summers is a Japan Times award-winning writer with a Masters Degree in Creative Writing from Bath Spa University. He is the founder of With Words which runs online courses in haiku and tanka poetry. Alan's work appears in *Haiku in English: The First Hundred Years* (W. W. Norton 2013).
Website: www.withwords.org.uk   Blog: http://area17.blogspot.com

John Terry is a persistent weed who by chance has taken root in Bristol and has proved impervious to herbicide. He's delighted that Dru chose to illustrate *Redwings*, and loves her wonderful shivering cat in *I See You* (written for a 4 year old who asked: *Can cats see the wind?*)

Cathy Wilson started writing poetry in her mid-forties, after which her previous lives started to make more sense. The natural world and especially its birds are frequent subjects in her work. Published in several anthologies, Cathy is a part-time library assistant, and a poetry tutor for the WEA in Bristol